Hypno Games For Hypno Junkies

By
Sarah Carson
Shawn Carson
and
Jess Marion

HypnoGames For HypnoJunkies

For further information please contact Changing Mind Publishing at 545 8th Avenue, Suite 930, New York, N.Y. 10018

 # Introduction and Welcome

Hello and welcome to the fun world of HypnoGames!

We can assume that as you have purchased this book you are either a proud, fully fledged, upstanding member of the "HypnoJunkie" community, or someone with a curious desire to become a true and deeply committed "HypnoJunkie"!

For us, our journey to becoming incorrigible "HypnoJunkies" began when we woke one day to find that our entire lives were surrounded with swinging watches, hypno-spirals, Milton Erickson purple leisure suits and that we were peppering every other sentence with "...That's Right…"

We quickly realized that a trance-formation had occurred and so we embraced our deep change and our newly found "HypnoJunkiness" by continuing to play with hypnosis long after our clients and students had returned home. Our love affair grew and developed with the three of us frequently playing hypnosis games deep into the night (with "TranceWars" being the ultimate battlefield for victory and glory!)

Over the years we have collected, developed, played, taught and enjoyed many HypnoGames and this book is a collection of some of our favorites.
We hope you enjoy playing them as much as we do!

Sarah, Shawn and Jess

How to use this book

▶ This book is divided into 5 sections; Convincers, Partner, Conversational, Movement and Group games. Each section has between 5 and 9 different games.

▶ On each page you will find the steps of the game, a mini "script" idea and a "Tips and Tricks" section for additional ideas, extended versions, and any safety points of which to take note.

▶ We suggest you gather a group of friends/fellow hypnotists together, or just one other person and simply begin by dipping into the treasure trove of games and selecting the one that draws your attention!

And most importantly...

Have FUN...
... FUN...
... FUN!!!

Convincer Games

Enjoy convincing your partner that something wonderfully hypnotic is happening.

Have fun allowing your unconscious mind to come out and play!

An old favorite...

Book and Balloon

Hold out your left hand palm up, and you right hand thumb up, like this... That's right, now close your eyes and imagine... I'm going to place a heavy book on your left hand like this [gently press your palm on theirs], and I'm going to tie a helium balloon to your thumb here, so it begins to pull upward into the blue sky... and another book, pressing down... and another balloon floating... [continue with more books and balloons]... now open your eyes... Wow, that's the power of your unconscious mind, it can literally create reality for you!

1. Have your partner hold out their hands, one palm up, one thumb up

2. Ask them to close their eyes

3. Tell them you are placing heavy books in one hand

4. Tell them you are tying helium balloons to the thumb of the other hand.

5. When their hands have moved down and up, ask them to open their eyes and look...

Tips and Tricks:
1. Make sure your partner has no shoulder problems or similar issues!
2. Get them to straighten the palm-up arm so more weight rests on the shoulder. (This tires the arm!) Allow them to keep the thumb-up arm a little bent so it doesn't tire.
3. Gently press down on the palm each time you 'place a book'. Gently tug up on the thumb each time you 'tie a balloon there'
4. Change you voice tone so it sounds 'heavy', when you talk about the books, and lighter when you talk about the balloons

Fire Hose Arm

Stand with your arm out at shoulder height. Keep it strong while I press down on your arm

Now imagine your arm is like a firehose, starting at your core and gushing out of your arm. Notice how strong it is now!

1, Ask you partner to stand and hold one arm out at shoulder height.
2. Ask them to keep their arm strong while you press down on it. Their arm is likely to show some resistance but will usually move downwards.
3. Ask your partner to imagine they have a fire hose inside them and that the water starts at their core and gushes out of their arm.
4. Add embedded suggestions about the strength of the water.
5.Push down on your partner's arm and notice the difference...all through the power of the unconscious mind!

Tips and Tricks:
 1- This is a classic convincer. Use compliance and embedded suggestions to enhance the experience.
2- Follow up the experience by suggesting that if your partner's unconscious mind can have a direct impact on the body, just imagine what an impact it will have when used as a ally to make lasting changes.
3- Make sure your partner has no shoulder neck or back issues before doing this!

A very old induction based on the body's natural magnetic energy...

Magnetic Hands

Did you know your body creates its own natural magnetic field? I'd like you to begin gently rubbing your hands together like this... [demonstrate]... that's right... take a look at your hands as you do, perhaps you can begin to see the magnetic field that you are creating, or perhaps not yet.... Separate your hands by a couple of inches and focus your attention on the space in-between... gently move your hands a little closer, now a little farther apart...

as you do you will begin to feel the magnetic field attracting your hands together... the magnetic field is running through this hand, through this arm, through your body, back down this arm, and this hand... begin to feel the flow of the field and as you do, notice yourself beginning to relax, allowing the magnetic field to lead you into trance... that's right...

1- Ask your partner to gently rub the palms of his hands together. This creates static electricity in his palms.

2. Ask them to move his hands a couple of inches apart and gently move them closer, then further apart and "feel the energy field"

3. Using suggestion, lead them to have 'magnetic hands' that are attracted to each other.

4. Link the suggestion of magnetic hands to suggestions for trance.

Tips and Tricks:
1. The trick to this induction is to have your partner focus his/her attention on the unusual feelings in the palms of his/her hands. This focus will allow your hypnotic suggestions to go to work.
2. Look out for signs of trance and incorporate what you see into your suggestions "I notice the magnetic field has begun to change your blinking, as it takes you into a magnetic trance..."
3. As a variation, you can suggest that his/her magnetic hands are anti-magnetic, meaning pushing each other apart.

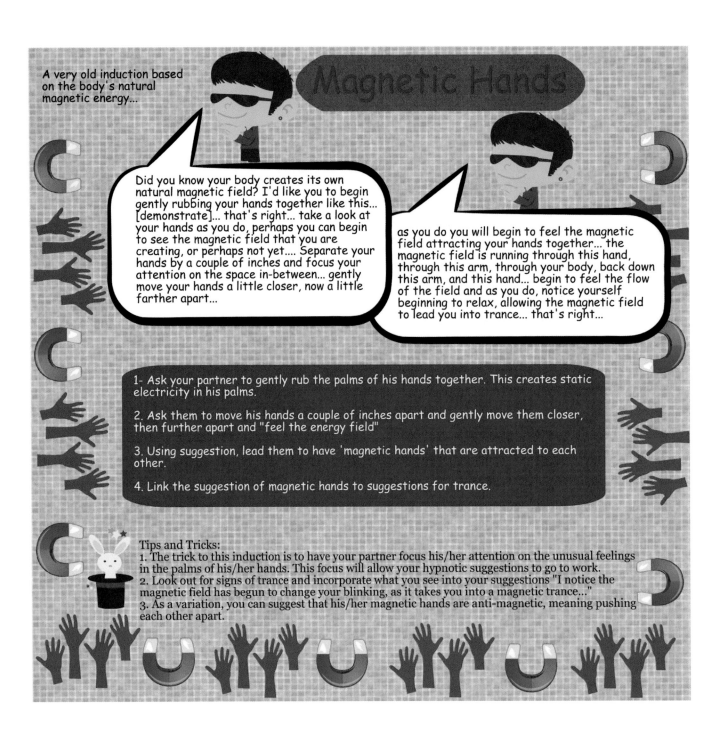

The Twist Around

Please stand and raise your left arm. Now twist around to your left and notice how far you go. Great...now close your eyes and imagine raising your arm and twisting, but this time you go further. Let's do this again...now imagine you are made of rubber and twist around 3 times! Now open your eyes and really twist around and notice how much further you go!

1- Ask you partner to stand with his feet shoulder width apart.

2- Ask him to raise one arm to about shoulder height and, keeping his feet still, twist around as far as he can. Ask him to make a mental note of how far he twisted. Now untwist and face you.

3- Ask him to imagine "in his mind's eye" raising his arm and twisting around, but this time twisting further. Do this twice going further each time.

4- Ask him to imagine that he is made of rubber or is a cartoon and to imagine twisting around 3 full turns. Remind him to "untwist".

5- Ask your partner to open his eyes, raise his arm and to really twist around.

6- Notice how much further your partner has gone and remind him about the power of the unconscious mind.

Tips and Tricks:
1- Make sure that your partner has no back, neck or shoulder issues.
2- When your partner is imagining you can often see slight movements of twisting. This is great!
3- Ask them to let you know when the have imagined "untwisting" each time by nodding their head.

CAUTION

The Human Pendulum
Using the mind/body connection to find the truth!

During any trance induction where the subject is standing, make suggestions of stability, and be prepared to support or catch them if necessary.

Stand with your feet shoulder width apart and close our eyes... thank you. I'm going to ask you a question; you don't need to answer out loud, in fact it's better if you don't. I'd just like you to notice which way your body leans. Is your name Fred?... Now open your eyes, which way did you feel yourself lean?... Let's do it again, close your eyes, now are you wearing a red shirt? Open your eyes, which way did you lean? Isn't it amazing that your body tells you the answer?!... Let's try a question you don't consciously know the answer to. Close your eyes... and as you're beginning to fully appreciate the power of your unconscious mind and the amazing things it does for you...are you making new connections?

1. Ask your partner to stand and close their eyes. Be prepared to support their balance if needed.
2. Ask them a yes/no question they know the answer to, "Is your name Fred?", and to notice which way their body sways. Ask them to open their eyes.
3. Ask them to close their eyes again and ask a few more yes/no questions until it's clear their body has an unconscious 'yes' lean and a 'no' lean. Ask them to open and close their eyes between each question.

Tips and Tricks:
1. This is a fun way to communicate with the unconscious mind. Asking your partner to open and close their eyes between questions 'fractionates' the trance experience. They will go deeper each time.
2. This will be a trancey experience for them, so feel free to layer in positive suggestions as you go.
3. At the end they will be in a deep trance state so you can move straight into a more formal trance.
2. Suggest they can stand strong and balanced, but also be prepared to support them if needed (very occasionally someone will sway off-balance).

Partner Games

Enjoy playing these 9 different games with a partner.

Take turns leading your partner into trance and let the fun begin!

Becoming One

Shortcut to Trance Nirvana...
Shortcut to Trance Nirvana...
Shortcut to Trance Nirvana...
Shortcut to Trance...
Shortcut to Trance

Sit comfortably and close your eyes...[induce a light trance using any induction]...as you are sitting there, I would like you to notice the breath entering and leaving your body, breathing in...oxygen that becomes part of your bloodstream and is carried round your body... breathing out... carbon dioxide that becomes part of the atmosphere... and as your continue to relax INTO the chair, notice your skin opening to the room around you, your skin breathing in and out... feel your hands on your legs, sharing energy... the warmth of your hands moving into your legs... and the warmth of your legs moving into your hands...that's right [as your partner relaxes further] and it's interesting to realize that everything your are is being exchanged with the world around you, new cells growing... old cells being released...you and the world are one... so that you can begin to feel...now... your skin touching your clothes...becoming one... merging... with the quantum field of the Universe as you are.. relaxing...releasing...becoming... one...more breath...

1. Lead your partner into a light trance

2. Begin to make suggestions that he is becoming one with his surroundings and the rest of the world

3. This induces a deep trance state of oneness, a sort of Trance Nirvana

4. While in Trance Nirvana, offer your partner positive suggestions

Tips and Tricks:
1. The key to this game is to start with simple, easily verifiable effects, such as feeling his hands on his lap, feeling his clothes on his body, and slowly build the suggestions
2. Pace your partner's experience by noticing the degree of relaxation he show as the trance deepens, only offer more complex suggestions as his trance deepens

Razor's Edge Induction

This induction was used in the 1946 movie The Razor's Edge with Tyrone Power.

Please hold the coin lightly and gently, and especially comfortably between you thumb and forefinger... Put all your attention on the coin, look at it... now... feel the temperature of the coin in your fingers... as you listen to my voice... feel the... weight... how light... reflects... off the coin... no need to pay attention... to your body... relaxing... as you are... feeling the coin... and when the coin slips away... falling... but not before... the coin... your fingers... dropping... now... that's right...

1. Ask your partner to lightly hold a coin between her thumb and finger.
2. Lead her to focus all her attention on the coin, the way it feels, looks, its weight and so on.
3. As she begins to go into trance (catalepsy, relaxation of facial muscles, change in blink rate etc.) reflect and suggest relaxation.
4. As the trance deepens suggest that when the coin drops she will close her eyes and 'go into trance'
5. When the coin drops, she will close her eyes, deepen the trance and proceed with suggestions.

Tips and Tricks:
1. Begin by simply keeping your partner's sensory attention on the coin, switching between visual, auditory and kinesthetic.
2. Trance will develop automatically. It doesn't matter whether she ever drops the coin and closes her eyes into 'formal' trance. As trance develops verbally reflect back whatever you see (e.g. 'body relaxing, eyes blinking').
3. Use the natural trance to make suggestions. initially these can be about relaxation, then move on to the change work.
4. If she doesn't initially drop the coin, you can suggest she will drop it when the change is complete.

The Visual Induction

Shhh.... No words...

Shhh...   Shhh...   Shhh...

Shhh...   Shhh...

Shhh...

1- Sit so your partner can see you clearly

2- Match her breathing and/or blinking

3- Slowly go into a comfortable eyes open trance, and watch to see if she follow

4- Once you see trance in your partner slowly raise your hand, then lower it to signal time to close their eyes

Shhh.... No words...

Shhh...   Shhh...   Shhh...

Shhh...   Shhh...

Shhh...

Induce trance without saying a word by using your physiology.

At first you mirror your partner, this is called 'pacing'.

Then you begin to lead them into trance...They become the mirror!

Tips and Tricks:
1. Your partner's unconscious mind will pick up on your trance signals and will begin to create the same experience in them. This is thanks to mirror neurons.
2. If he/she doesn't follow you immediately, go back to pacing for a few moments.
3. When hypnotic rapport is present this is a quick way of inducing trance.
4. Practicing this induction will dramatically increase your success rates with verbal inductions because you will be using this type of non-verbal induction as well.

Picture This... Trance

Take a moment to settle you mind and just breathe...now take a look at your picture and allow your eyes to slowly scan...find one detail that interests you for a moment...now find another...and as you do allow yourself to step inside and experience this from the inside out...

1. Select a picture, angel card, tarot card you like

2. Take a slow breath and gaze at the card with soft eyes

3. Scan the image until you find some detail that interests you

4. Imagine stepping inside the image to experience it from the inside out

Tips and tricks.
1. Make sure you have a positive picture to look at, one that makes you feel good.
2. Use all the senses to enhance the experience while inside the image.
3. Use present tense language when leading your partner e.g "see what you are seeing, hear what you are hearing" etc

James Braid's Crystal Induction

"I'm going to show you this crystal... and I would like you to focus.. your gaze on it he crystal... noticing... as you relax... now... the gentle movement... of the light... taking you into a comfortable state... that's right... and as the crystal moves closer to your... going into trance...

now...that's right eyes closing...going deeper..."

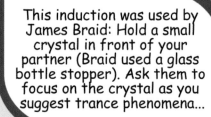

This induction was used by James Braid: Hold a small crystal in front of your partner (Braid used a glass bottle stopper). Ask them to focus on the crystal as you suggest trance phenomena...

TIPS:
1. Hold the crystal above your partner's eye level (this will tend to tire their eyes)
2. You don't need to tell them to go into trance, just suggest relaxation, comfort and other trance phenomena
3. Watch out for blink rate changes, facial relaxation, and other signs of trance.
4. Take your time, let them get nice and sleepy!
5. When you see your partner going into trance, move the crystal toward them, suggesting their eyes will close as you do, and that they will go deeper...
6. Begin your suggestions

Starry Night

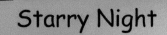

Imagine you are in a beautiful place where you can see the night sky filled with stars. Close your eyes and roll your eyes up to look directly above you at the stars

...begin to scan the beautiful night sky watching the different stars twinkling and glowing. And as you do you notice one star in particular. Bring that star down now closer to you ...allow it to be right in front of you and roll you eyes back down

so you can look at the the star. Begin to feel the energy and message the star has for you. Now take this energy of this star inside

1. Imagine above you a night sky filled with stars
2. Close your eyes and roll them back in your head to look at the stars above your head
3. Select one stars that draws your attention
4. Bring that star down in from of you (as you roll your eyes all the way down)
5. Feel/experience the energy/light/message of that star
6. Allow the star/enery/message to merge with you.

Tips and Tricks:
1. This can induce a nice deep trance that can be used for fun, relaxation or change work.
2. The metaphor of the star and it's energy can be used as healing energy, a positive resource, connection to something greater than oneself.
3. Don't keep your clients eyes rolled back in the head for too long as it can be uncomfortable.

The Rainbow Trance

Sit comfortably and close your eyes. I'd like you to imagine that you... see a rainbow in front of you, each band of color clear, red, orange, yellow, green, blue and indigo-violet. You begin moving toward the rainbow and are surprised to find yourself entering the red of the rainbow. As the red light surrounds you, you begin to feel a red warmth move through your skin and into your body, your warm breath relaxes you completely. And as the red surrounds you and the warmth spreads through your body, you begin to feel passion to pursue your dreams. Now I don't know if this passion is something you feel regularly, or perhaps it's been some time since you felt it, but you notice it begin somewhere inside, and then to spread like the red light through your bloodstream, being taken to every part of your body...[continue with red and the other colors in order]

1. Have your partner sit comfortably and close his eyes
2. Have him imagine moving through a rainbow, color by color
3. Have him see the color, then also feel the color. This 'synesthesia' is hypnotic
4. Suggest associations for each color
5. Your partner will go into a rainbow trance

Red: Warmth, Breath, Passion, Enthusiasm, Motivation

Orange: Creativity, Playfulness, Exploration

Yellow: Clarity, Thought, Memory, Decisions

Green: Balance, Nature, Health, Growth

Blue: Cool, Peace, Understanding

Indigo: Wisdom, Intuition, the Unconscious

Violet: Spiritual mastery, Love, Inspiration

Tips and Tricks:
1. The key to this game is the multi-sensory experience
2. Become used to the associations between each color and the sensory experiences associated with that. You can use the above script as a guide or develop your own
3. If you prefer, you can play this game as part of a 'walking' trance, i.e. have your partner walk through the rainbow colors
4. Once your partner has gone into trance you can offer positive suggestions or move into another game

The Gourmet Trance

Now I'd like you to imagine your favorite food in front of you...let me know when you see it clearly... what do you see?... What do you smell?   What else?... Now take a bite [spoonful]... what do you notice first? What do you taste?... What else?... What happens next?... So first [repeat sequence]...

1. Induce trance with any induction
2. Have your partner see their favorite food
3. Have them imagine smelling and tasting the food

Tips and Tricks:
1. Use a light trance at first and ask your partner to describe their experience
2. The description should be in sequence; first I see X, then I see/smell Y, then I see/smell/taste Z from the plate or dish into the mouth, down the throat, into the stomach, into the bloodstream etc
3. Then induce deeper trance and describe the sequence, in order, to your partner
4. This Gourmet Trance can be used to experience the effects of alcohol or drugs. We strongly advise against doing so for medical and legal liability reasons.
5. This may increase the subject's desire for that food, so do not use this with subjects who have eating disorders, or a tendency to gain weight!

Ascending the Tree of Life

From Tree of Life Coaching by Shawn Carson

1- Simply ask your partner the questions listed, ascending in the order shown in the diagram
2- Give your partner plenty of time to consider each question. They do not need to answer out loud and it is better if they don't as you ascend the tree
3- When you reach the top of the tree, if your partner is in a good place simply ask them, "and where are you now?" to reground them

10. Where and when is the source of all of this?

9. Aside from that, what's everything else you haven't been aware of?

8. Who taught you that? When did you learn that?

7. What's important to you about that?

6. What should you do? What can't you do?

5. What is everything you're aware of inside and out? What does all of that mean in the bigger picture?

4. What are you feeling, now? Where do you feel that in your body?

3. What are you thinking, what pictures are you making inside, now?

2. What does that mean, now?

1. Where are you, now? When are you, now?

Tips and Tricks:
1. It is important to build a strong rapport, to 'hold the space' for your partner, and to give them time to consider each question
2. If your partner reaches the top of the tree and is not in a good place, return to the ninth point, "And aside from that, what's everything else you haven't considered?" to give them the opportunity to find a positive state
3. For a longer experience, when they are in a good state at the top of the tree, descend through all the points in the reverse order

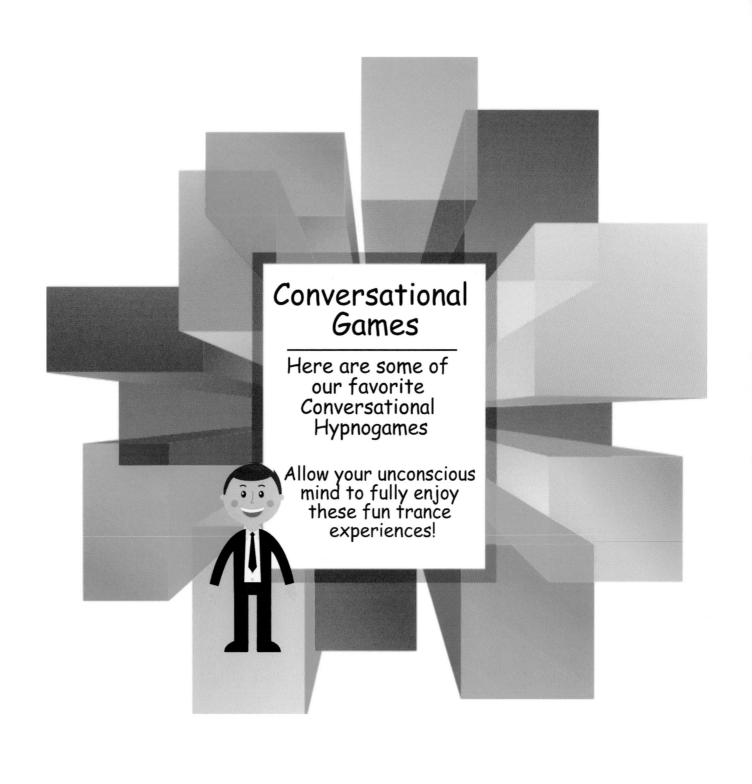

Conversational Games

Here are some of our favorite Conversational Hypnogames

Allow your unconscious mind to fully enjoy these fun trance experiences!

Symbolic Realities Game

This game is inspired by the work of James Lawley and Penny Tompkins, developers of Clean Language.

That's (insert partner's word for good feeling) like......what?

And when "x" what kind of "x" is that?

And when "x" where is "x"?

What needs to happen to "x"?

Can that happen?

What's the relationship between "x" and "y"

What happens next?

Steps
1- Have 3 people: 1 facilitator and 2 participants

2- Facilitator associate participants into an unambiguously positive state

3-Alternate between participants using Symbolic Modeling questions

4- Build a strong positive shared trance landscape

Tips and Tricks:

1- Clean Language keeps facilitator out of the subject's metaphor. Stick to only clean questions and always use the subject's exact words.
2- This will build a deep trance that is based on metaphors so it will not make conscious sense
3- Ask the relationship question of both participants so as to link the metaphors for them
4- This is a great way to learn and practice Clean Language

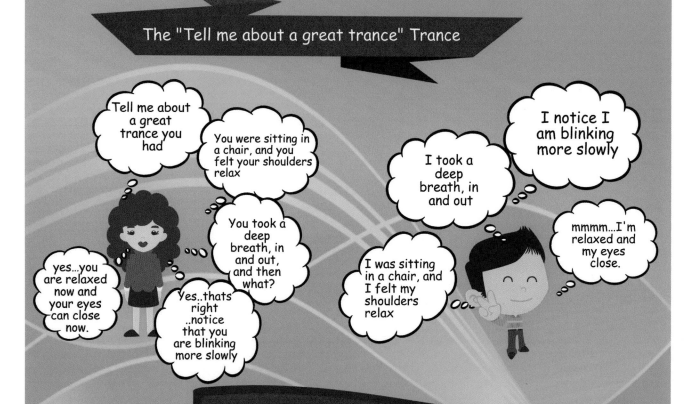

The "Tell me about a great trance" Trance

1. Ask your partner to tell you about a great trance experience
2. Echo back their phrases in your best hypnotic voice
3. Notice trance beginning to occur
4. Switch to present tense language and confirmation their experience with "that's right" and "yes" etc

Tips and Tricks:
1. This tends to induce deep trances so have them sit down or if standing, suggest their feet and legs will support them.
2. Use lots of repetition of your partner's responses and embedded commands to deepen the experience for them.
3. Modeling their blink rate/breathing/posture. This will enhance the trance!

The Knot Game
A great trance induction for polarity responders who talk to themselves

I would like you to notice how comfortable you are feeling now

I'm not... feeling comfortable... now

As you are going into trance...

I'm not... going into trance... now

And not going deeper ... now

I'm not... not... going deeper... now

1. Give your partner instructions for going into trance, e.g. "You're going into trance now," using your best trance voice
2. Your partner denies the instruction but with the same tonality/voice-speed as the instruction and always leaving a pause after 'not', "I am not... going into trance now"
3. Because the unconscious does not deal well with negation, your partner is effectively repeating your instructions (even while consciously saying the 'opposite')

Tips and Tricks:
1. The trick is to ask your partner to leave a short pause after the word 'not'. This 'embeds' the trance instruction
2. Make sure your partner uses 'trance tonality' and a slow speed. This is really important.
3. Ask your partner to add the word 'now' at the end of their sentence.
3. When you are confident that your partner has 'got it', ask them to begin speaking inside their mind.
4. If using this with a client (it's great for 'polarity responders' as well as those with a lot of self-talk as they can speak any thoughts in the same way, "I'm not... going into trance"

This induction game comes directly from the works of Milton Erickson, John Overdurf, and Shawn Carson

What's everything you can be aware of right now that you haven't been paying attention to about going into trance?

That's right, and what about that can take you deeper?

Inductive Langauge	Deductive Language
Everything	Only
Anything	One Thing
All	This
Everytime	That
Anytime	Here
Always	Now
Everywhere	Each

1- Invite your partner to notice an expansive range of their current sensory experience. Use inductive language to find something they were not previously aware of, something that will lead them deeper into trance.

2- Use deductive language to focus her attention down to specific experiences about going into trance.

3- Enjoy expanding and contracting awareness all the way

down...

into...

trance

Tips and Tricks:

1- This works through implication. Over time you expand or contract your partner's awareness to embed suggestions that the experience is leading to trance.

2. It's a great game for the hypnotist to practice inductive and deductive language

Goal Repetition Induction Technique

1- Ask your partner to come up with a Goal. Help him to state the Goal in one single statement that is evocative for them, e.g. "I am flowing into creativity"

2. Ask him to begin repeating the Goal, one word for each breath, "I - - AM - - FLOWING - - IN - -TO - - CREATIVITY"

3. When he is comfortable, begin to weave a trance induction into his Goal, "I - you - AM - you are - FLOWING - flow in - TO - to one - ..."

Tips and Tricks:
1. This is a great game for hypnotists to practice free-form trance language in a controlled environment. Use tonality, sometimes say nothing then occasionally speak over your partner.
2. Slow your partner down enough so you have time to speak between his/her words.
3. The main thing is for the hypnotist to have fun, use puns (the unconscious mind loves puns).
4. For your partner it's like a double induction and can lead to deep trance.

We first heard this from Caty Shannon who learned it from Steve Gilligan who learned it from...?

Movement Games

These 5
Hypnogames all
involve movement.

Enjoy playing these
games with a partner
and get ready to go
deep inside!

The brain doesn't know the difference between something deeply imagines and the real world.

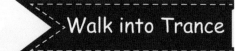

Each step closer to the chair takes the "you" in the chair deeper into trance...

1-Stand your partner 10 feet away from a chair

2-Have your partner imagine they can see themselves in the chair, going into trance

3-Ask them to take a step toward the chair and describe something they are noticing about the 'Trance' version of themselves in the chair

4-Repeat step 3 a number of times, suggesting that each step toward the chair takes the "them" in the chair deeper into trance

5-Your partner will drop into trance as they get closer to the chair

6-Have them sit in the chair and go even deeper into trance

Tips and tricks
1- This trance produces deep trance experiences, so suggest that your partner's legs and feet will remain strong and will support them
2-Walk at the side of your partner and watch them closely at all times
3-Use repetition of your partner's responses and embedded command to deepen the trance experience

CAUTION

The Invisible Shelf

Surface as a metaphor

Close your eyes and relax completely... In a moment, but not yet, I'm going to gently lift your hand, and place it on an invisible shelf in front of you... Now begin to slooowwwly move your hand along the shelf, noticing its contours, its shape, how it rises and falls as you move your hand along the shelf... Now this shelf represents your [golf game], as your hand moves left you are moving into the past, to your earlier days as a golfer, notice how the shelf rises and falls, and what those represent... now move your hand into the future, and notice how the shelf changes...

1. Lead your partner into a gentle trance. This can be eyes open or eyes closed

2. Ask them to feel an invisible shelf in front of them. Encourage them to run their hand along the shelf and notice its shape

3. Use the shelf as a metaphor for their future and past in a specific context. Notice how the shape and contours of the shelf correspond to the issue over time

Tips and Tricks:
1. This is a great technique for teaching your partner arm catalepsy. Most people can feel the 'invisible shelf' very easily even if they have more trouble with catalepsy
2. Ask your partner's permission to touch their hand and arm before you start
3. Use 'ambiguous touch' at the beginning to help your partner 'find' the shelf. Encourage your partner to move their hand slowly but smoothly

NAPA* Induction

*It's called the NAPA induction because we created it on a wine tour of Napa Valley in California!

Do you mind if I borrow your hand? Thank you. So we are just going to ask that hand to go into trance first... just about like... that... now one thing you may not know is that your hand has two directions, one that leads deeper into trance... let's find that one first [moving hand to left]... are you going deeper into trance or... deeper? OK I guess we've found it, so the opposite direction [moving the hand right] will lead you out a little... great... now let's see how deep this trance goes [left]... [right] are you feeling relaxed now? great! let's go back in [left]... [etc. etc.]

1. Induce catalepsy in your partner's hand and arm using ambiguous touch

2. Tell them that moving their hand in one direction will take them deeper into trance, and in the other direction will bring them more out of trance. You are going to find out which is which. You can use up-down or left-right, it doesn't matter.

3. Move their hand an inch in one direction and ask them if they went deeper into trance or less deep?

4. Validate whatever they say, and show them the opposite direction has the opposite effect (it will).

Tips and Tricks:
1. The trick to this induction is that catalepsy IS trance. When they are in catalepsy they are already in trance!
2. Once you have established which direction is deeper and which is less deep, you can easily fractionate by gently moving their hand backward and forward. This can lead to really DEEP trances!

5. Use the 'deeper into trance' direction to take them into trance. Begin the suggestions.

Shadow Hands

Look at your partner's hand, begin to notice every detail of that hand...the shape...the shadows... the lines..the tiny creases and movements...Now...imagine that your partner's hand is in fact your hand ...That hand is part of you...this hand here ...your hand is feeling comfortable and relaxed and I wonder how easy and comfortable it is as I gently touch your hand...

This is a game for 3 participants. 2 players and one hypnotist.

1. Sit facing each other and ask each person to raise their right hand palm down to about waist height.

2.Tell each player to begin to focus on the other person's hand and to begin to notice all the details.

3. Lead the two players into an open eye trance and begin to suggest that the other person's hand is in fact their hand.

4. Begin to tell one player that you are touching their hand (while touching the other players hand) and notice what the first players response is!

Tips and Tricks:
1. Ask the players to sit opposite each other and make sure that their hands are not resting on the arm of the chair.
2. Ask the players to keep their eyes open for this game and suggest they can still go deeply into trance.
3. Begin to induce confusion as to who's hand is who's by switching between players names and using this/that/your/her hand interchangeably.

The Mesmerist!!!

Or the 'Scooby Doo Induction'

Stand there... now gaze into my eyes... that's right... I'm going to exert my hypnotic influence, please rest assured my assistant are there to catch you should you fall backward into trance so you are perfectly safe. And as you gaze into my eyes, and you feel yourself falling under the hypnotic influence I will begin the hypnotic finger waving, just like you see in the movies.... and you feel yourself swaying... that's right, deeper and deeper...

1. Have your partner stand facing you, with their eyes open. Have a couple of reliable assistants stand behind them to catch them if necessary.
2. Tell them you are going to put them into a deep hypnotic trance!
3. Stare into their eyes, wave your hands and fingers in 'hypnotic passes' until their eyes close. Be theatrical!
4. Offer positive suggestions about going deeper into trance, and positive suggestions for change, then bring them out of trance in the usual way.

Tips and Tricks
1. Choose a partner who has already shown hypnotic responsiveness
2. Make sure your partner feels very comfortable with you, and very safe in the exercise. Have reliable people behind them to catch them, and be prepared it catch them if they fall forward!
3. Make strong eye contact. Match their blink rate then speed up your own blink rate, they should follow.
4. Look for their natural tendency to sway, and begin to match this with you movements and 'hypnotic passes'. Begin to change the rate of your own movements till they follow. Finally change the amount you move; this will increase their sway until they topple into trance.
5. Remember, your partner is offering you control, be very careful you are offering them only positive and ethical suggestions

Group
Games

Here are 5 games to
play in a group setting.

You can modify each
game for larger or
smaller groups.
Get ready to trance
out now!

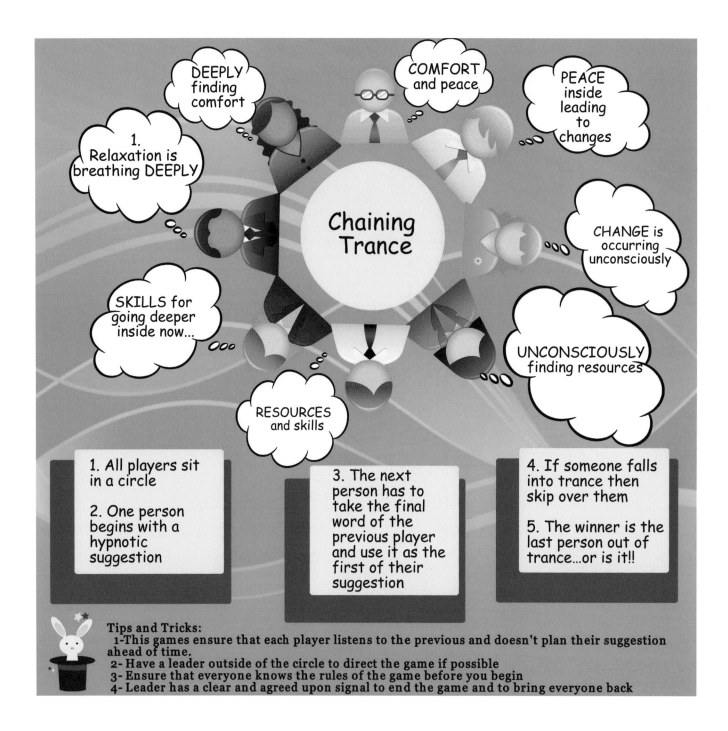

The Double Induction

You are feeling relaxed ...

and beginning to drop inside...

and deep comfort and ease...

finding a place of quiet...

you are able to gather deep insights...

As you begin to relax, I wonder how many new ways...

to find resources and solutions...

you can breathe yourself deeper into trance...

This is a game for 3 people

1. Sit either side of your trance partner. Set a timer, a gentle ringtone works best, or agree upon a visual signal between Hypnotist One and Two so it is clear when to wrap up the trance.

2. Hypnotist One begin to induce a trance.

3. Hypnotist Two begins to join in with the trance, weaving words with Hypnotist One.

Tips and Tricks:
1- Experience this game with Hypnotist One and Two sitting in different positions, i.e sit facing your trance partner, sit slightly behind, sit with one hypnotist in front and one hypnotist behind. Notice how each experience is different for the trance partner.

2. If one of the hypnotists speak a second language, experience dropping into your second language part way through the trance. Notice how it is different for your trance partner.

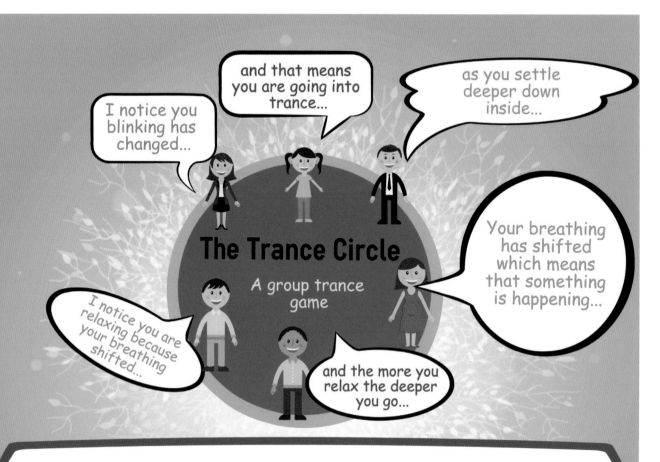

The Trance Circle

A group trance game

1. For three or more players. Everyone sits in a circle
2. First person makes a trance suggestion to their neighbor in the circle
3. Second person makes a suggestion to their neighbor
4. The third person makes a suggestion to their neighbor
5. And so on until someone closes their eyes and are 'out'. This continues until only one player is left!

Tips and Tricks:
1. This is a great opportunity to practice basic skills such as hypnotic gaze, voice variability, embedded suggestions and so on
2. Feel free to 'play to lose'! The first loser gets the deepest trance!

The Instant Story Game

1. This is a game for 4 or more players.

2. One person is storyteller and three of the listeners give the topic and two items for the storyteller to include.

3. Decide who will give the positive theme and which two players will give an item.

4. On the count of 1...2...3 call out the theme and the objects (this way it is very random)

5. The story teller goes into trance and begins to weave a story that includes all 3.

6. Watch as the group goes into trance!

Tips and Tricks:
1- Remember to use hypnotic language, embedded suggestions and metaphors in your story.

2- For more fun you may add more items and a second theme!

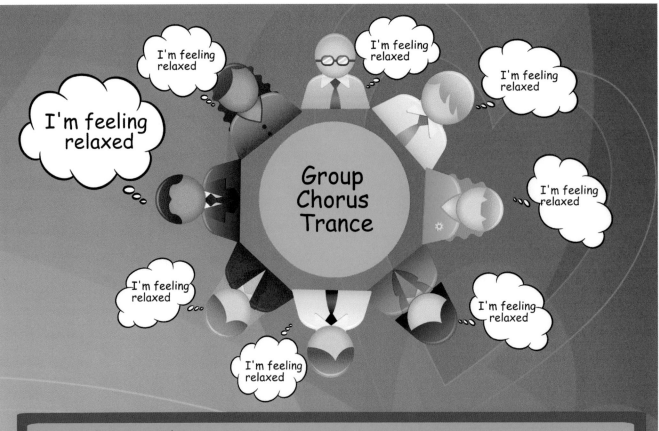

1. Sit in a circle

2. One person gives a positive trance suggestion and the group "choruses" it back.

3. Taking it in turns to give the positive suggestion, the group continues to go around the circle.

4. If someone drops into trance, then skip over them.

5. The winner of the game is the person who stays out of trance the longest....or is it!!!

Tips and Tricks:
1- Have a leader outside of the circle to direct the game if possible
2- Ensure that everyone knows the rules of the game before you begin
3- Leader has a clear and agreed upon signal to end the game and to bring everyone back

The Congratulations Trance

1-This trance experience can be for a birthday, celebration, congratulations or simply for fun!

2-The person receiving the trance sits on a chair in the center.

3- One person (leader) starts by inducing a light trance.

4-One by one, every member of the group joins the trance and gives positive wishes.

5-The leader brings the trance to a close and brings the hypnotee back.

Tips and Tricks
1-Use a variety of volumes so all can be heard
2-Participants can move in and out of the circle so all have an opportunity to give a "hypnotic gift".
3- Remember t have Fun..Fun Fun!!!

Trance ★ Wars

Imagine the ultimate trance challenge that pits your hypnotic skills against another master hypnotist!!

Rules: First person to close their eyes loses... (and wins!)

"You're going down...deep deep down"

"Bring it on Buddy"

"You're taking the "T" train to Trancetown"

Each person takes turns as hypnotist then as hypnotee.

In each round the time for the induction increases. So in the first round each hypnotist has 1 minute to induce an eyes closed trance. Round two is 2 minutes. Round three increases to 3 minutes.

Continue until one person drops deeply into an eyes closed trance. The winner can then give positive suggestions.

Tips and Tricks:
1- This game has the added benefit of creating highly responsive hypnotic subjects. It will also give you the chance to explore your own experiences of deep trance.
2- Both you and your opponent will go deeply into trance well before someone's eyes close. You will learn how to enjoy deep eyes-open trances
3- If you want to win go into a self directed trance before you partner hypnotizes you.

Other Publications by the authors:

The Swish: An In Depth Look at this Powerful NLP Pattern. (NLP Mastery Series)
Shawn Carson and Jess Marion

The Visual Squash: An NLP Tool for Radical Change. (NLP Mastery Series)
Jess Marion and Shawn Carson

The Meta Pattern: The Ultimate Structure of Influence for Coaches, Hypnosis Practitioners, and Business Executives. (NLP Mastery Series)
Sarah Carson and Shawn Carson

The BEAT Coaching System. (NLP Mastery Series)
Shawn Carson and Sarah Carson

Quit: The Hypnotist's Handbook to Running Effective Stop Smoking Sessions.
Jess Marion, Sarah Carson, Shawn Carson

Keeping the Brain in Mind: Practical Neuroscience for Coaches, Therapists, and Hypnosis Practitioners.
Shawn Carson, Melissa Tiers

Deep Trance Identification: Unconscious Modeling and Mastery for Hypnosis Practitioners, Coaches, and Everyday. Shawn Carson, Jess Marion, John Overdurf

Tree of Life Coaching: Practical Secrets of the Kabbalah for Coaches and Hypnosis and NLP Practitioners.
Shawn Carson

I Quit: Stop Smoking Easily Through the Power of Hypnosis.
Jess Marion, Sarah Carson and Shawn Carson

For further information please contact Changing Mind Publishing at 545 8th Avenue, Suite 930, New York, N.Y. 10018 or visit www.bestnlpnewyork.com

Printed in Great Britain
by Amazon